ANATOSAURUS

by Janet Riehecky
illustrated by Diana Magnuson

THE CHILD'S WORLD

MANKATO, MN

*Grateful appreciation is expressed to Bret S. Beall,
Curatorial Coordinator for the Department of Geology,
Field Museum of Natural History, Chicago, Illinois,
who reviewed this book to insure its accuracy.*

PAPERBACK EDITION
ISBN 0-516-46251-2

Library of Congress Cataloging in Publication Data

Riehecky, Janet, 1953-
  Anatosaurus.

  (Dinosaurs)
  Summary: Describes the physical characteristics and
probable behavior of this plant-eating duck-billed
dinosaur.
  1. Anatosaurus—Juvenile literature.   [1. Anatosaurus.
2. Dinosaurs.]   I. Magnuson, Diana, ill.   II. Title
III. Series: Riehecky, Janet, 1953-   Dinosaur books.
QE862.Q65R52   1989   567.9'7   89-22063
ISBN 0-89565-545-4

ANATOSAURUS

Strange, huge creatures once roamed the earth. They were the dinosaurs!

4

Most of the dinosaurs were gentle plant eaters. But not all of them! Some were fierce meat eaters.

Plant-eating dinosaurs needed a defense
from meat eaters. Some were armored,
almost like tanks. A meat eater would
have a hard time trying to take a bite out
of an armored dinosaur.

Other plant eaters were simply too big
and strong. A meat eater would usually
look for smaller, weaker prey.

Some plant-eating dinosaurs had weapons to fight an attacker. A meat eater would have to be pretty hungry to take on a many-horned dinosaur.

What a meat eater really looked for was
a dinosaur that couldn't put up much of a
fight.

One such dinosaur was the Anatosaurus
(ah-NAT-uh-sawr-us), which means "duck
reptile." It was a gentle plant eater whose
mouth was shaped like a duck's bill. It
wasn't too big, and it didn't have any
troublesome armor or horns. Scientists
know a lot about this dinosaur because
they have found two Anatosaurus mummies. The mummies still had skin on them,
and one of them even had the remains of
its last meal in its stomach!

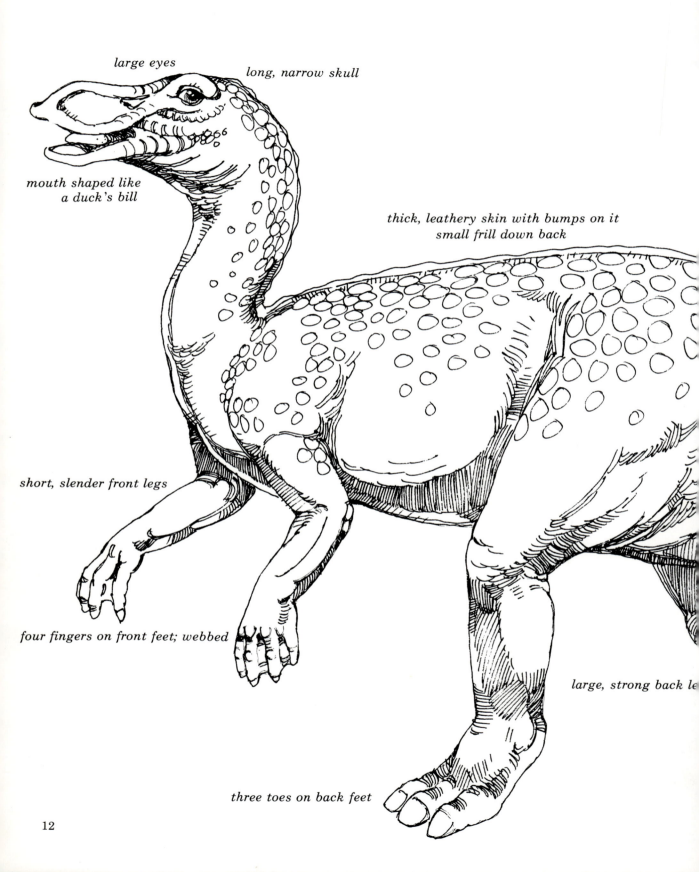

large eyes

long, narrow skull

mouth shaped like
a duck's bill

thick, leathery skin with bumps on it
small frill down back

short, slender front legs

four fingers on front feet; webbed

large, strong back le

three toes on back feet

12

The Anatosaurus could grow eighteen feet tall, thirty-three feet long, and could weigh as much as a very large elephant. That may sound huge to you, but it was just an average size for a dinosaur. And to a hungry Tyrannosaurus, it was just the right size for dinner!

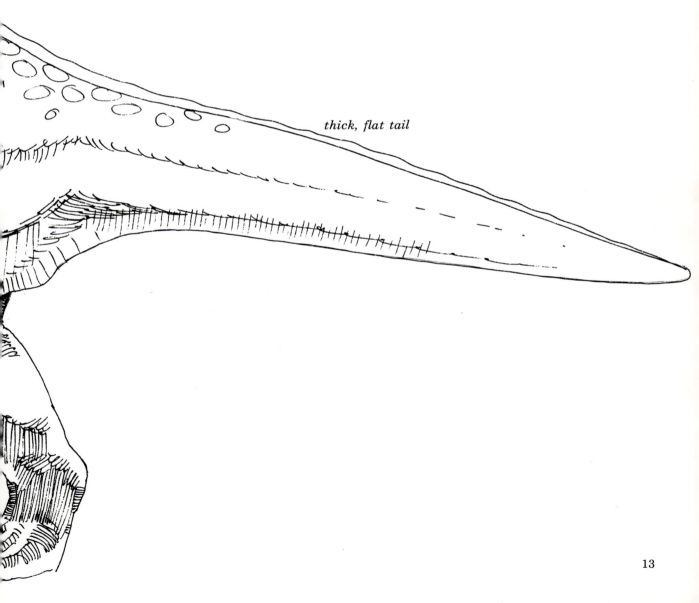

thick, flat tail

When a Tyrannosaurus wanted an Anatosaurus for dinner, it usually wouldn't have too much trouble. The Anatosaurus wasn't made for fighting. Its feet were webbed, sort of like a catcher's mitt, and didn't even have sharp claws. Its skin was thick and leathery, like a crocodile's. The skin was tough, but not thick enough to stand up to the sharp teeth of a Tyrannosaurus.

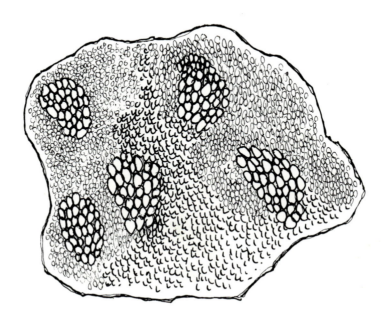

The mouth of the Anatosaurus wasn't built for fighting either. Its snout was shaped into a broad beak, like a duck's bill. It didn't have any teeth at all in the front of its mouth—but it had plenty in the back. The Anatosaurus had as many as 2000 teeth, stacked in rows four deep, in its back jaws. As its teeth wore out, they were replaced by the ones underneath. But its teeth were not very sharp. They were made to grind up plants, not fight off an attacker.

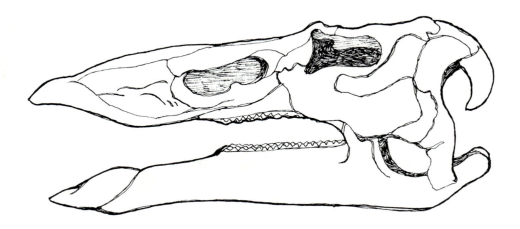

Many scientists think the Anatosaurus had one advantage over most meat eaters. They think it could swim. The Anatosaurus probably spent much of its time in lowland areas near rivers and lakes. If a meat eater came too close, the Anato-

saurus could make a quick escape. Scientists think its thick, flat tail propelled the Anatosaurus quickly through the water and that its webbed feet made great flippers.

When the Anatosaurus wanted a meal, it wasn't too fussy about what it ate—twigs, shrubs, pine needles, fruit, and seeds—all of these sounded good. The Anatosaurus needed to eat a lot of food every day. It could scoop up mouthfuls of food in its big, shovel-like mouth—the more the better. It could even store food in its bulging cheeks to have a second mouthful ready when it was done with the first.

Even while eating, though, the Anatosaurus had to stay alert. Fortunately, it
had sharp eyesight, keen hearing, and a
great sense of smell. Nothing could sneak
up on it!

If the Anatosaurus sensed danger was
near, some scientists think it puffed air
into a loose flap of skin over its nostrils.
The flap would blow up like a balloon and
probably make a loud noise. That might
scare away a little meat eater.

Of course, a big meat eater wouldn't care about a little noise and a scary face. That's why the Anatosaurus usually liked to have a lot of friends nearby. Scientists think the Anatosaurus lived in large herds. Many Anatosaurs traveled the countryside together, finding food and enjoying each other's company. Most meat eaters would avoid a large group. It would be easier to attack an Anatosaurus without friends.

Sometimes Anatosaurs were caught away from the herd. Some might wander away looking for food. Some might become injured and fall behind. If a Tyrannosaurus found one then, the Anatosaurus could only try to run away. Scientists think it was a swift and graceful runner, so sometimes it would succeed in getting away—but sometimes it wouldn't!

The Anatosaurus didn't spend all its time just trying not to get eaten. Scientists think it was a loving parent. They believe the Anatosaurus made a nest, carefully watched over its eggs, and took special care of its babies after they hatched. It brought them food and kept them safe from the meat eaters.

Anatosaurs lived on the earth for millions of years, but sixty-five million years ago, they and all the other dinosaurs died. Yet they are still being hunted today—not by meat eaters, but by wishful thinkers.

Deep in the heart of South America and Africa, there are legends of living dinosaurs. People say real dinosaurs roam the tropical forests, far from civilization. Scientists say this could not possibly be true. They say the people who think they've seen dinosaur-like creatures are mistaken. But that hasn't stopped a lot of people from hunting for them.

No one has found one yet—and brought proof of it back. Scientists say they never will. But if you want to hunt for dinosaurs—plant eaters or meat eaters—there are two places you can find them—in books and in your imagination.

 ## Dinosaur Fun

Scientists have learned a lot from the Anatosaurus mummies they have found. The dinosaurs' bodies were preserved because they were dried out before they decayed.

Flowers can be preserved in the same way. You can try it yourself. You will need:

— a shoe box
— freshly cut, blooming flowers
— 5 cups of white cornmeal
— 1-1½ cups of borax

1. Mix the cornmeal and borax in the shoebox. The mixture should be about 1 inch deep. If it's not deep enough, make more of the mixture to add to the box.
2. Lay the flowers on top of the mixture. Sprinkle some of the mixture on top of the flowers to just barely cover them.
3. Put the box in a dark place, such as a closet, for about 3 weeks. (Check on them from time to time.)
4. When the petals feel dry and crisp, gently take the flowers out of the mixture. Put your "mummified flowers" in a pretty vase to display them.